Painting

with watercolors

Paige Henson

The Rourke Press, Inc.
Vero Beach, Florida 32964

ART CREDITS:
© Corel: page 5; C. Beyl, Kingfish Studios: pages 21, 22, 24, 25; Jon DiVenti, Kingfish Studios: pages 11, 18, 29; Bob Hochgertel, Kingfish Studios: pages 10, 13, 16, 19, 20; Charles Reasoner: pages 4, 14, 15, 23

PHOTOGRAPHY:
Glen Benson and East Coast Studios

PRODUCED & DESIGNED BY:
East Coast Studios, Merritt Island, Florida

EDITORIAL SERVICES:
Susan Albury

ACKNOWLEDGEMENTS:
East Coast Studios would like to thank Gardendale Elementary School, Merritt Island, for their assistance in this project.

Library of Congress Cataloging-in-Publication Data

Henson, Paige, 1949-
    Painting with watercolors / by Paige Henson
        p. cm. — (How to paint and draw)
    Includes bibliographical references and index.
    Summary: Provides techniques and advice on painting with watercolors and suggests several projects to try.
    ISBN 1-57103-312-2
    1. Watercolor painting—Technique Juvenile literature. [1. Watercolor painting—Technique. 2. Painting—Technique.] I. Title. II. Series: Henson, Paige, 1949- How to paint and draw.
ND2440.H46 1999
751.42'2—dc21   99-30659
                                                           CIP

Printed in the USA

Contents

CHAPTER 1

Painting with Watercolors

If you've never painted with **watercolors** (WAH ter KUH lurz), you're in for a pleasant surprise. This is because watercolor paint is thin and transparent, and light shines through from the paper beneath it, giving your art a special, light-filled look no other paint offers. Watercolors mix, blend, and dry quickly, and cleanup is easy. Perhaps best of all—watercolors are handy and portable. In fact, you can paint just about anywhere there is water available to mix your colors.

The History of Watercoloring

The first watercolors were probably used by ancient Chinese artists more than 2,000 years ago. Most were painted for spiritual purposes, and special lettering called **calligraphy** (kuh LIH gruh fee) was often added to the art.

In the early 19th century, watercolors again became popular when they were used to paint vast outdoor scenes called landscapes. These landscapes showed the enormous power of nature through pictures of majestic mountains, stormy seas, and immense skies.

This watercolor painting by William Turner was created during what was called the Romantic Age (ro MAN tik AJ).

CHAPTER 2

What You'll Need

1 Watercolors are sold in tubes like oil paints, in pressed blocks of color arranged in small plastic pans, or in cakes of color in miniature boxes. All forms of the paint must be mixed with water before using. If you go outdoors to paint with watercolors, like many artists do, remember that you'll need to bring water in a container for mixing.

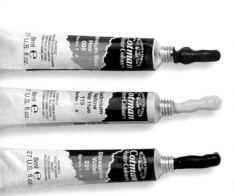

2 Use a #2 pencil for sketching out your picture before painting it and an eraser for slipups on your sketch OR to erase pencil marks that show through the paint.

3 Choose light-colored paper like white, off-white, gray, or soft brown.

5 Brushes of various sizes and an old toothbrush to use for **spattering** (SPA ter ing).

6 Two medium-sized jars of water—one for loading paint on the brushes; one for cleaning the brushes.

7 Something to use as a color-mixing palette.

8 A sponge to blot up excess moisture on your brushes as you paint.

9 Rags or paper towels for spills.

CHAPTER 3

Let's Start Painting!

The texture of the paper you choose will also make a difference in the way your painting looks. Using smooth, flat paper like the pages of this book, will give you a whole different painting than using a textured paper. The textured paper will hold water and color in its "hills and valleys" to create an interesting, shadowy effect for your painting.

Stretching Paper

If you are not using heavyweight watercolor paper, prevent your finished watercolor painting from curling up around the edges when it dries by stretching it before you paint.

STEP 1 Place the paper on a board and using a very wet sponge, wipe over the paper from left to right, starting at the top. Make sure the paper is nice and flat with no air bubbles.

2 Stick gummed brown tape along all four sides of the paper. When the paper dries, it will dry flat.

Color

Primary colors (PRI mair ee KUH lurz) are red, blue, and yellow. Blending any two of these three basic colors will give you different colors, called **secondary colors** (SEH kuhn dair ee KUH lurz). From these primary and secondary colors, you can mix just about any other color you want. When you mix colors for watercolor painting, however, never mix more than three together or you will end up with a muddy color.

Mix colors on a paper plate, the lid of your paintbox, or any other white, flat surface. Experiment with mixing until you get just the color you want.

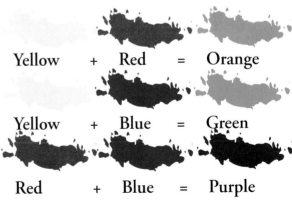

Yellow + Red = Orange

Yellow + Blue = Green

Red + Blue = Purple

Leaving Some Areas White

Instead of painting with white watercolor, you can leave areas unpainted that you wish to be white. Part of learning to paint with watercolor is planning your work ahead of time so that the white of your paper becomes an important part of your finished painting. This works best when you are preserving areas with defined shapes or outlines, such as those in this umbrella. White areas can also serve as highlights and reflections of light.

Besides using white by leaving some areas unpainted, you can try lifting color from your paper before it dries to expose the white of the paper beneath it. Use a cleaned brush that you've dried thoroughly with a paper towel, or try a tissue to lift off the color. Both techniques take some practice, so be patient!

Keep in mind that large areas of white such as snowy scenes will require more than the white of your watercolor paper to appear realistic. Think of it: have you ever seen flat, white snow? Of course not! Snow, especially on a day that the sun shines on it, sparkles with pastel colors of many hues—blues, pinks, and even yellows. Watercolor is the perfect **medium** (MEE dee uhm) to paint beautiful snow scenes.

Light and Shadows

Observe that your shading (seen on an object), and shadowing (seen off the object), are at the opposite side of where the original light source hits the object. Avoid using black for shades and shadows. Instead, try adding darker hues of cool colors like blues, greens, and purples.

Laying a Wash

One of the first things you need to know is how to "lay a wash." This means covering your paper with one flat, transparent color. A **wash** (WAHSH) gives you a nice, finished background to paint over. Here's how:

First, choose or mix a color for your wash. Mix only a little paint with lots of water. The wash color should be a light tone so that other colors can be easily painted over it.

STEP 1
Wipe your paper with a damp sponge.

STEP 2
Starting at the top of the paper, paint a strip of the wash color from left to right across the paper.

STEP 3
Notice that each time you paint a strip of color, some of the paint has puddled at the bottom of the strip. Quickly and smoothly "catch" the paint puddle and brush it away quickly, so your wash color will be smooth and even.

STEP

4 Repeat Steps 1, 2, and 3 until you have come to the bottom of your paper. If your wash is too light, you may go over it again.

You may have to practice laying a wash before you are able to do it easily, but after you learn this technique, you will be on your way to becoming an expert watercolor artist.

Secret Brush Techniques of the Pros

Three fun techniques every good watercolor painter should know are:

Dry brushing

To use **dry brush technique** (DRI BRUHSH tek NEEK), dampen your brush just a little and load it with as much color from your palette as you can. If the brush won't pick up color easily, wet it just a little more, but not *too* much! Sweep your almost-dry brush across your paper, moving from left to right. Notice that as the brush moves right, the color fades out and leaves interesting-looking open spaces that create a nice texture for skies and other things.

Spatter

Spattering paint on your paper with an old toothbrush creates an interesting, finely dotted texture. First, using plain paper, cover up the areas of your painting that you don't want spattered. Mix up some thick paint by using less water than usual; dip the toothbrush bristles in the paint mixture; then flick your thumb against the bristles to spatter on the paint.

Wet-on-wet

Wet-on-wet technique (WET on WET tek NEEK) will surprise you every time! Wet some areas of your paper thoroughly with a clean cloth, sponge, or large brush. Quickly, before the wet area dries, dab it with the tip of a wet brush loaded heavily with color. See how the paint magically "flowers" out on its own?

15

CHAPTER 4 Painting Landscapes & People

Composition and Planning Your Painting

Composition (kahm puh ZIH shun) is the arrangement of all the pieces or elements in your painting. Some artists create a balanced painting with a central subject. Good composition begins with deciding which way to turn your paper—horizontally (left to right like the horizon), or vertically (up and down).

Then decide where you want the main object in your picture to be. For example, if the main object you will be painting is a tall tree, try turning your paper vertically (up and down) and place the tree near the bottom of the page or a

little to the left or right. See how much more interesting this composition will be than just trying to center everything in the middle of your page?

Decide on a background color and lay your wash as described on page 12. After the wash has dried, lightly sketch in all the elements of your picture.

Painting Flowers and Trees

Landscapes are outdoor scenes that feature such things as trees, grass, flowers, water, rock formations, deserts, and other elements found in nature as well as buildings such as barns and churches.

Landscapes are great for watercolor painting. Try these simple techniques:

Trees

The colors you use for trees will depend on the season. Trees in winter will look bare with only a skeleton of trunk, branches, and smaller twigs showing. Summer trees, on the other hand, will be a vivid green with fewer branches showing. The leaves on autumn's trees will be turning warm brown, orange, red, and yellow.

Try painting the tree's "skeleton" first with a fine-tipped brush and black paint. When this is dry, use your round brush to add a blob of wash to create foliage.

Use a tissue to lift or remove some of the color so your tree has an interesting variation of tones. You might add some short dabs of paint that represent individual leaves.

Flowers

First, sketch out your overall flower shape with a light-colored crayon. Add petals using a fine-tipped brush (try not to load too much water and color on your brush to paint delicate flower petals!). You may want to add a darker tone of the color you choose where the flower meets the stem. When the paint on the basic flower has dried, add details on the flowers that will be seen close-up. Flowers growing together in the distance can be merely suggested by painting a wash of bright color in a line. You can dab at the still-wet color with a tissue to create an even softer look.

Try Painting a Friend

STEP 1

Sketch everything lightly in pencil—do not press hard. Lay a wash for the skin and while this is still wet, lay in a wash for the hair, allowing the color from the skin to merge with the hair. This will help the hair from looking like a wig when finished.

STEP 2

Using a darker mix of color, paint in shadows along the side of the head and under eyes, eyebrows, nose, and chin. Add life to your painting by using washes of blues, browns, greens, and purples. Avoid using pure black.

STEP 3

Paint should be applied much more carefully now. As you build up the dark areas, keep the paint transparent so that all the work you have done so far can show through.

When the painting is completed, go back and pull out highlights by using water and a stiff brush.

19

STEP 1

Sketch everything lightly in pencil—do not press hard. Lay a wash for the skin and while this is still wet, lay in a wash for the hair. Yellow ocher was used for this picture. Allow the color from the skin to merge with the hair.

STEP 2

Using a darker mix of color, paint in shades along the side of the head and under eyes, eyebrows, nose, and chin. Avoid using pure black. Instead use washes of browns, greens, and reds. Carefully paint in the shapes of the nose, lips, and ears, etc.

STEP 3

Work carefully as you build up the dark areas, keeping the paint transparent so that all the work you have done so far can show through.

Now go back and pull out highlights by using a little water and a stiff brush. Or you can paint "back in" using opaque white watercolor.

CHAPTER 5

More Terrific Techniques

Crayon pictures become even more wonderful works of art if you paint over them with watercolors. The paint "slides" off the waxy crayon marks and puts color in the spaces all around the objects you've drawn and colored in. Try this and you will be surprised at the results.

Mystery Painting

Using white construction paper, draw a picture with crayons of several colors, making sure to press down hard. Now, paint over the lines of your drawing with black watercolor. This creates a mysterious "night time" effect.

Now You See It...

Another fun idea is to draw a picture of something on white construction paper with a white crayon. Can't see your picture? Paint over your drawing with watercolor, and your white art will appear like magic!

Painting with Salt

Adding salt to your watercolor painting creates cool-looking spots and sparkles. Try this:

STEP 1 Paint in only the areas where you want to add a spotted effect.

STEP 2 Sprinkle the painted areas with salt BEFORE the paint dries.

STEP 3 After it dries, brush the salt away and paint in the rest of your picture.

PROJECT

Create Your Own Watercolor Techniques

The great artists of the world have not thought of everything! Use your imagination to think of ways to add interest to your watercolor painting. Perhaps you could introduce a new way of adding texture. Perhaps you could develop a way to let the paint flow down your paper to create interesting shapes. As you continue to work with watercolor and its special properties, you will soon find many artistic ways to solve watercolor problems, express yourself, and create the images you want. Your paintings will be original and yours alone!

Try Painting a Fiery Dragon

STEP 1 Sketch everything lightly in pencil—do not press hard. Lay in washes of color, covering the background and the dragon.

2

Add green to the dragon's head, legs, wings, and edges of scales. Add brown lines to his belly. Paint in the hills and foreground with greens and browns. Note that a shadow has been painted under the dragon, and orange has been added to the flames and marshmallows.

STEP

3

Paint a brighter green wash over the dragon, except for his belly. Using brown/green paint, create a shadow on his belly and underside of his tail. Add red to flames and smoke around marshmallows and nostrils.

Try Making Your Own Portfolio

Keep your paintings safe in a cool portfolio!

STEP 1

Select two pieces of board, maybe in your favorite color. The boards should be the same size and at least as stiff as cardboard. Lay them side by side and stick a piece of wide tape down their length to hold them together.

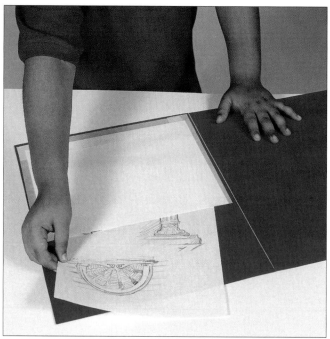

STEP 2

Inside, place a piece of paper close to the bottom of the right board. Place a piece of tape along the bottom of the paper and its two sides, sticking it to the board. This makes a "pocket" in which to place your art.

Now you have a
handy portfolio you can
take anywhere!

PROJECT

Tissue Paper Watercolor

Use bright colored tissue paper torn into small pieces.
Arrange the torn bits on a piece of white paper laid flat. With a
spray bottle of water, spray the paper, wetting the pieces
thoroughly. Next, wet a paintbrush and go over the colored
tissue paper to help "milk out" the color. Remove the wet pieces
and notice that the paper beneath has been stained with color.

CHAPTER 6

Cleanup

Cleaning up watercolor is easy! Just wash paint from your hands, your palette, and your brushes. To protect your paintbrush tips, don't stand your brushes in water, tip-side-down and leave them there. Instead, store them handle-side-down in a jar, or dry the brush tips and store them flat in a drawer. Remember, watercolor brushes should never be soaked in water overnight!

Do this...

...not this!

1 Be sure your watercolor paintings are completely dry before storing them. You might need to lay them flat in a safe place to dry for a few minutes.

2 Close the top of your watercolor box to preserve your paints. If you use watercolors in tubes, remember to replace each cap!

3 Use a sponge to wipe off any surfaces that may have been splashed with watercolor.

4 Put everything away and wash your hands. You might use an old tackle box or something similar to store your paint and paint tools together.

Cool Tips

Watercolor paints in tubes sometimes harden and the paint cannot be squeezed from the tube. If this happens, try running the tube under warm water to soften the paint.

PROJECT

Paint a clothesline with some bright, colorful clothes hanging out to dry. Try to use the different techniques you have read about in this book to create interesting patterns and textures.

Glossary

calligraphy (kuh LIH gruh fee) — from a Greek word that means beautiful writing; calligraphy was an early art form used for the fancy lettering of books and papers

composition (kahm puh ZIH shun) —the arrangement of objects, shapes, color and other elements in a painting

dry brush technique (DRI BRUHSH tek NEEK) — a watercolor technique that uses very little water mixed with watercolor paint to create a special streaked effect

medium (MEE dee uhm) — the substance, such as watercolor, oil, charcoal, etc., used in creating art

primary colors (PRI mair ee KUH lurz) —red, yellow and blue; primary colors cannot be created from other colors.

romantic age (ro MAN tik AJ) — a time in the 18th and early 19th centuries when many artists and writers used freedom of form and style as opposed to more formal styles; the Romantics created art that emphasized nature and things having to do with the common man.

secondary colors (SEH kuhn dair ee KUH lurz) — two primary colors mixed together to create either orange, green, or purple

spattering (SPA ter ing) — flicking wet watercolor or other paint from the bristles of a toothbrush to make a splash of dots on a painting

wash (WAHSH) — a layer of thin watercolor, usually a transparent background

watercolors (WAH ter KUH lurz) — an art medium composed of ground-up colors with a gum binder that is to be mixed with water before using; watercolor is available in tubes or pans.

wet-on-wet technique (WET on WET tek NEEK) — a watercolor technique of touching a brush filled with color to a paper already very wet to create a special flowery effect

Index

Further Reading

- Brookes, Mona, *Drawing with Children*, G. P. Putnam's Sons, 1996.
- Cummings, Pat, *Talking with Artists*, Simon & Schuster, 1992.
- Cummings, Pat, *Talking with Artists Vol. II*, Simon & Schuster, 1995.
- Davidson, Rosemary, *Take a Look: An Introduction to the Experience of Art*, Viking, 1994.
- Johnson, Cathy, *Painting Watercolors*, North Light Books, 1995.
- Kohl, Maryann, *Preschool Art*, Gryphon Press, 1994.
- Martin, Judy, editorial consultant, *Painting and Drawing*, Millbrook, 1993.
- Martin, Mary, *Start Exploring Masterpieces*, Running Press, 1991.
- *Learning to Paint in Watercolor*, Barron's Educational Series, 1997.
- Robb, Tom and Phillips, Phoebe, *Start Now in Watercolor*, Aurum Press, 1992.
- Thompson, Kimberly Boehler and Loftus, Diana Standing, *Art Connections*, GoodYearBooks, 1995.